WHO IS SHE?

She is a daughter. She is a best friend. She is a pocketful
of light. She is a spark of something good, getting brighter,
a dream grown large, the right thing at the right time.

Her spirit is the first thing people notice. Her mind always
has a mind of its own. Her heart, though it has sometimes
been hurt, bears a strong resemblance to a daffodil:
it always flowers again.

So she wakes with anticipation. She finds new hills to climb.
And everyone agrees that the very fact of her in the world
means there is still so much good to come.

Who is she? She is me. She is you.

I am her.

"AS A WOMAN,
I HAVE NO COUNTRY...
AS A WOMAN MY
COUNTRY IS THE
WHOLE WORLD."

VIRGINIA WOOLF

The map to where she's going is written on her heart—
its roads and rivers are her dreams, her strength, her
confidence. The way is not always easy, but when she
takes a moment to notice the scenery, she sees that
it is always beautiful.

I am her.

She stood in the light,

turned a new corner,

and burst all at once

into bloom.

The branches above her,

the shadow at her feet

saw her newness,

gave it room.

"ADVENTURE IS A STATE OF MIND— AND SPIRIT."

JACQUELINE COCHRAN

She promises herself new places, different views, a chance to get lost. She infuses her day with wonder. She brings a notebook everywhere, notices the little things, gets a cup of coffee at a different café, takes the long way home. She discovers so much unexpected joy. She begins to love the journey.

I am her.

A phone call from an old friend, just when you needed it.
The sound after a snowfall. A perfect peach. A moment
of sheer confidence. Finding the right words. Feeling strong.
Knowing the answer. Green lights. New growth.
A compliment. Quiet time. Sudden laughter.

SOME FAVORITE
MINOR MIRACLES:

1

2

3

4

5

"IF SHE GOT
REALLY QUIET
AND LISTENED,
NEW PARTS OF
HER WANTED
TO SPEAK."

SUSAN ARIEL RAINBOW KENNEDY

She still speaks to the little girl who wanted to be an artist, a doctor, a poet, a woman who walked on the moon. She pays attention when that little girl talks, when she paints pictures of the clouds, when she draws something huge in sidewalk chalk. She makes her every day a place for old dreams and new dreams, dreams that tower and dreams that whisper.

I am her.

"KNOWING WHAT YOU WANT IS THE FIRST STEP TOWARD GETTING IT."

MAE WEST

wishes I've made:

wishes I will make:

wishes I haven't even admitted yet:

"Your playing small doesn't serve the world. There's nothing enlightened about shrinking so that other people won't feel insecure around you. We are all meant to shine..."

MARIANNE WILLIAMSON

She unfurls her wings. She speaks her mind. She is a beautiful parcel of boldness and grace, all wrapped together, brilliant. Shining. The more of her own light she allows to shine, the more those around her shine too. From high up, she imagines they must look like a constellation.

I am her.

"ON REFLECTION,
ONE OF THE THINGS
I NEEDED TO LEARN
WAS TO ALLOW MYSELF
TO BE LOVED."

ISHA MCKENZIE-MAVINGA

compliment practice:

Write down all the nice things people say about you. Choose at least one to believe every day.

Turn your light on.

Shine it out into the world.

Watch what happens next.

"...SELF-RESPECT HAS NOTHING TO DO WITH THE APPROVAL OF OTHERS..."

JOAN DIDION

She wants to be remarkable, wants a flash, a spark, a rare and wonderful spirit that everyone sees. But before all of that, she wants to respect herself. As is. Even the shaky parts. Because even the shaky parts have a brilliance to them that doesn't fade. She grows ever stronger in the life she has made.

I am her.

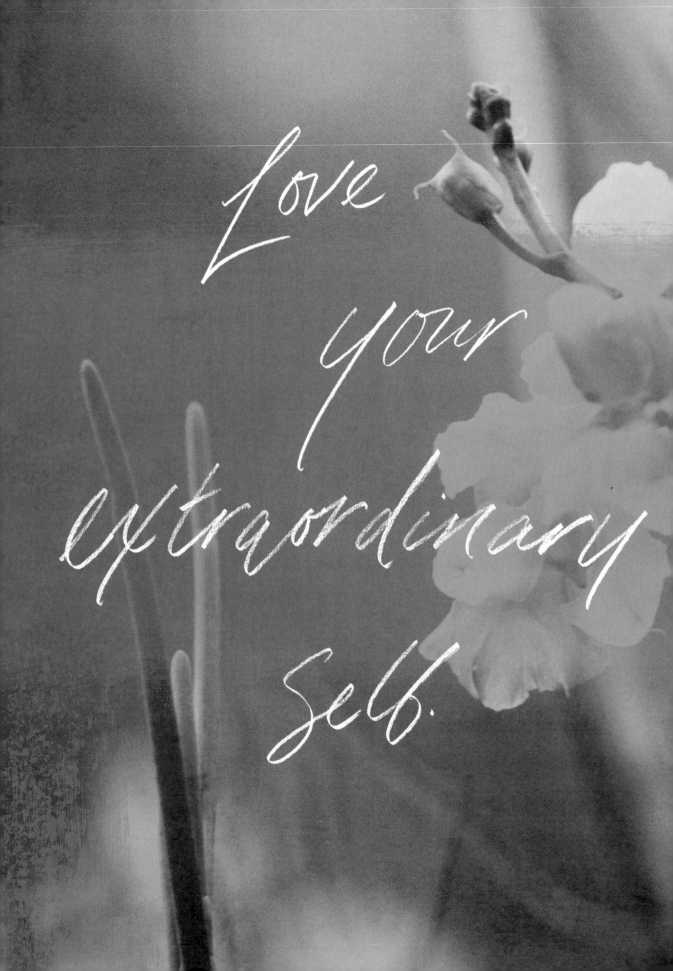

Love your extraordinary self.

"TURN AWAY FROM
THE WORLD THIS YEAR
AND BEGIN TO LISTEN.
LISTEN TO THE
WHISPERS OF YOUR
HEART. LOOK WITHIN."

SARAH BAN BREATHNACH

She lies awake and listens to what her heart has to say, hears it declare that this is the beginning of her own new year, and in this year...

She will:

She won't:

And she'll start:

"I read and walked for miles at night along the beach... searching endlessly for someone wonderful who would step out of the darkness and change my life. It never crossed my mind that that person could be me."

ANNA QUINDLEN

"...IT IS ONLY THE FIRST STEP THAT IS DIFFICULT."

MARIE DE VICHY-CHAMROND

There are some days, some tasks that seem like hills to climb. Lately, she does not mind them so much. She finds that once she begins them, she has more momentum than she had imagined. The muscles of her legs and the muscles of her mind crave these worthy challenges.

I am her.

"Change doesn't happen in the middle. It only happens when we venture over to the edge and take one small step after another."

KAREN SHERIDAN

The goal:

The steps:

The reasons:

"IT'S UP TO YOU TO

CHERYL STRAYED

MAKE YOUR LIFE."

"When I dare to be powerful, to use my strength in the service of my vision, then it becomes less and less important whether I am afraid."

AUDRE LORDE

She puts on the outfit that makes her stand tall, meets her own gaze in the mirror: resilient and capable and ready. There is nothing in this day that is too much for her. There is nothing she cannot meet with clear eyes and a willing heart and a strength that bubbles up inside her like a spring.

I am her.

"SEE EVERY DIFFICULTY AS A CHALLENGE, A STEPPING STONE, AND NEVER BE DEFEATED BY ANYTHING OR ANYONE."

EILEEN CADDY

"I need to take an emotional breath, step back, and remind myself who's actually in charge of my life."

JUDITH M. KNOWLTON

I GIVE MYSELF PERMISSION TO:

starting this very moment.

Write your own permission slip for the field trip you've been
needing, the dream you've been holding, the thoughts you
haven't allowed yourself to voice yet.

"IF YOU DON'T LIKE THE WAY THE WORLD IS, YOU CHANGE IT. YOU HAVE AN OBLIGATION TO CHANGE IT. YOU JUST DO IT ONE STEP AT A TIME."

MARIAN WRIGHT EDELMAN

She plans big, she gets to work, she has faith in her own momentum.
She knows that change doesn't happen all at once, but she welcomes it,
she prepares for it, she gives it fertile ground.

I am her.

"You gain strength, courage, and confidence by every experience in which you really stop to look fear in the face...You must do the thing you think you cannot do."

ELEANOR ROOSEVELT

Things that are true already:

Things to make true:

"I AM NOT A HAS-BEEN. I'M A WILL-BE."

LAUREN BACALL

And I will be:

(circle all that apply)

ADAPTABLE / ADVENTUROUS / AFFECTIONATE
ARTICULATE / ARTISTIC / ASSERTIVE / BALANCED
BRAVE / BRILLIANT / BUOYANT / CALM
CLEARHEADED / COMFORTABLE / COMMITTED
COMPASSIONATE / COMPETITIVE / CONFIDENT
CONSIDERATE / CONTENT / COOPERATIVE
COURAGEOUS / CREATIVE / CURIOUS / DECISIVE
DETERMINED / EAGER / ENERGETIC / ENTHUSIASTIC
EXCITED / FANTASTIC / FLEXIBLE / FOCUSED
FORGIVING / FULFILLED / GENEROUS / GRATEFUL
GROUNDED / HAPPY / HARDWORKING / HONEST
IMAGINATIVE / INDEPENDENT / INFLUENTIAL
INNOVATIVE / INSIGHTFUL / INSPIRED / INVOLVED
JOYFUL / KIND / LOVING / LOYAL / MOTIVATED
OPEN-MINDED / ORGANIZED / ORIGINAL
PASSIONATE / PATIENT / POSITIVE / PRODUCTIVE
RECEPTIVE / RELIABLE / RESPONSIBLE / SECURE
SELF-AWARE / SHINING / SPARKLING / STABLE / STRONG
TENACIOUS / UNFLAPPABLE / VISIONARY / WILLFUL

"I will not die an unlived life. I will
not live in fear of falling or catching fire.
I choose to inhabit my days, to allow
living to open me, to make me less afraid,
more accessible; to loosen my heart until it
becomes a wing, a torch, a promise."

DAWNA MARKOVA

Do
You

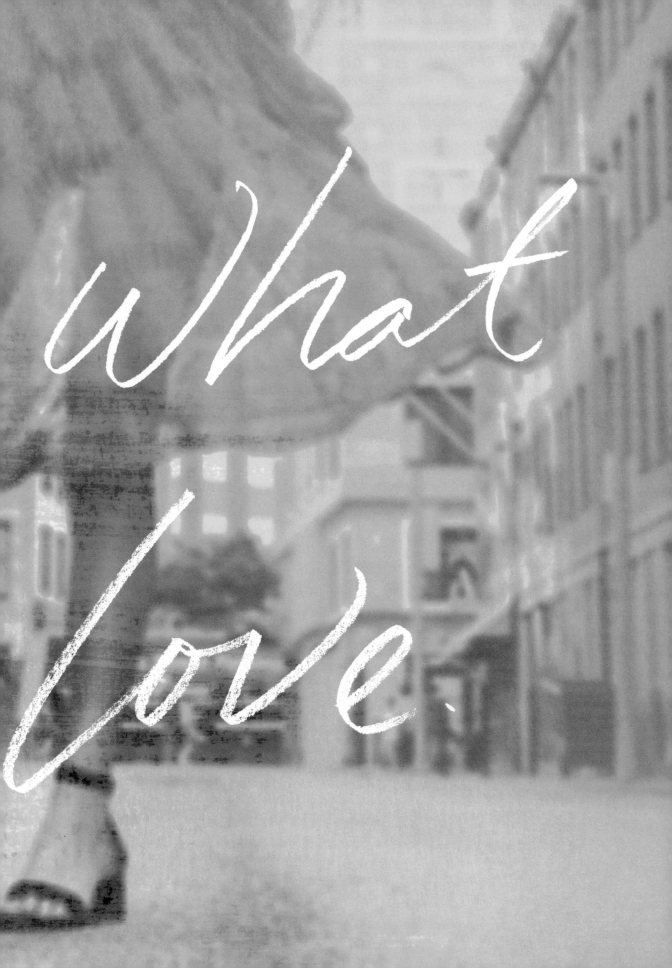

"FEMALE FRIENDSHIPS THAT WORK ARE RELATIONSHIPS IN WHICH WOMEN HELP EACH OTHER BELONG TO THEMSELVES."

LOUISE BERNIKOW

She keeps the dreams her friends forget. The ones that seem too big or too distant, or built for someone else. And when the moment is right, she returns them to their owners, and she reminds them what they've always known: we need each other. We reach the stars together.

I am her.

"The most beautiful people we have known are those who have known defeat, known suffering, known struggle, known loss, and have found their way out of the depths. These persons have an appreciation, a sensitivity, and an understanding of life that fills them with compassion, gentleness, and a deep loving concern. Beautiful people do not just happen."

ELISABETH KÜBLER-ROSS

"THERE IS TIME FOR WORK. AND TIME FOR LOVE. THAT LEAVES NO OTHER TIME."

COCO CHANEL

Time for work

These are the work projects that matter most:

Time for love

These are the passion projects that matter most:

"BE BOLD IN WHAT YOU STAND FOR."

RUTH BOORSTIN

"ALL THE WOMEN I KNOW FEEL A LITTLE LIKE OUTLAWS."

MARILYN FRENCH

They stay out late, they call each other at unexpected times, they give each other's wild ideas a place to grow. They make their own rules, and then they break them. They take risks, they ask for more, they grab onto the things they want and never let them go.

I am her.

"I WAS ALWAYS LOOKING OUTSIDE MYSELF FOR STRENGTH AND CONFIDENCE, BUT IT COMES FROM WITHIN. IT IS THERE ALL THE TIME."

ANNA FREUD

"EARTH'S CRAMMED WITH HEAVEN..."

ELIZABETH BARRETT BROWNING

She gets goose bumps from tiny, perfect things. Seeing the stars. Fruit trees in bloom. The scent of dinner from a neighbor's house, a phone call at the right time, a bar of exotic chocolate. She keeps a list of the gorgeous parts of the everyday: maple leaves, new perfume, the last bit of light before sunset. She adds to it all the time. She is rich with wonder.

I am her.

Today is a good day to welcome the unexpected, to give it some room, to let something marvelous unfold.

Today is a good day to write a love letter to your own bright future, your own best self, your own most dearly held dream.

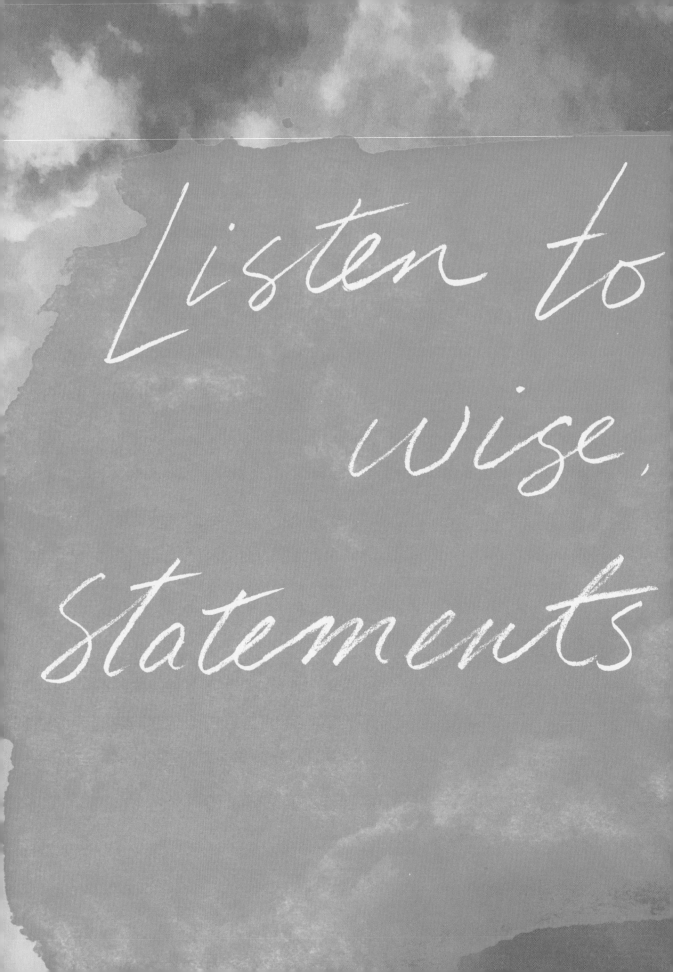

Listen to wise, Statements

the true, knowing of your heart.

Things to create:

Things to remember: